# ♦ All in a Day's Work

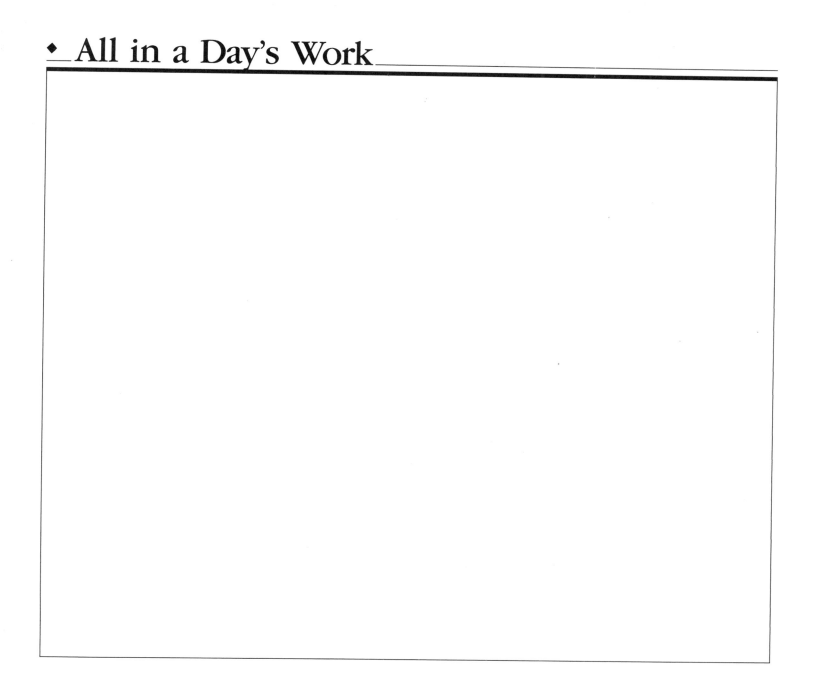

• • • • NEIL JOHNSON

# All in a Day's Work

• *Twelve Americans*
*Talk About Their Jobs*

**Little, Brown and Company** | BOSTON · TORONTO · LONDON

First edition
Library of Congress Cataloging-in-Publication Data
Johnson, Neil, 1954–
    All in a day's work : twelve Americans talk about their jobs /
Neil Johnson
        p. cm.
    ISBN 0-316-46957-2
    1. United States — Occupations.   2. Employees — United States —
Interviews.   3. Professional employees — United States — Interviews.
4. Work.   I. Title.
HF5382.J56 1989
331.7′00973 — dc20                                    89-32624
                                                          CIP

10   9   8   7   6   5   4   3   2   1

Joy Street Books are published by
Little, Brown and Company (Inc.)
BP
*Published simultaneously in Canada*
*by Little, Brown & Company (Canada) Limited*
Printed in the United States of America

For
Rita Hummingbird,
my love and my inspiration

◆ ◆ ◆

# ✦ Contents

# ◆ Author's Note

Each of these people interviewed here is unique. Their backgrounds, skills, and interests differ greatly. They have their own special ambitions, desires, and dreams. While the pilot was first inspired by flying with his father in the Idaho mountains, the restaurateur from Mexico was motivated by always wanting to do something for himself with his work. The journalist likes being a kind of "gatekeeper of information," while the police detective likes a job that can be unpredictable and exciting, and the social worker looks for work that allows her to "make a difference," even if it's temporary.

These diverse backgrounds and ambitions contribute not only to how each of these people feels and thinks at work, but also to how they feel about the job when they come home. Because each person I interviewed had such different experiences and hopes, I realized that two people working side by side at identical jobs would probably describe their work very differently. Each person defines the job in his or her own terms. That is why I felt that to truly understand work

and working, we had to meet the individual behind the job.

In selecting people for this book, I looked for individuals who were enthusiastic about their work, willing to talk openly about it, and who felt comfortable being photographed on the job. I tried to find people who had been at their jobs for several years, men and women who had some perspective on the choices and challenges they've faced over the years. In interviews, they described to me what they like and don't like about their jobs, how they got into their work, and, most important, why they stay in it.

In presenting their stories, I wanted not only to let these people describe their jobs in their own words, but also to actually show them at work — the pilot in his cramped cockpit high above the clouds, the farmer out in the wide-open fields, and the restaurant owner sweating from the heat in his kitchen.

Photography opens the door to these people's workplaces, and, if the photographer is patient, to their feelings as well. It allows us to see things that cannot be put into words. When the musician speaks of performing "in the middle of a whole mass of people," a photograph of him on stage in the midst of other orchestra musicians gives us some sense of how performing might feel. When the social worker talks about children learning how to care, a photograph of a hug evokes the feeling she's describing.

Twelve Americans, twelve jobs, twelve ways of making a living. In working on this project, I gained a great deal of respect for each of these individuals. They play music, solve crimes, and grow food to eat and cotton for clothing. They inform us, resolve our arguments, and keep our massive amounts of information organized. They prepare and serve us food, defend our country, and find shelter for those who have none. They heal us of disease and injury, build transportation for us, and educate us.

These people have generously opened up their lives and enriched my own life by allowing me to listen to their stories, consider their words, and watch them through the viewfinder of my camera. And for that I'm most grateful.

# STAN SAVANT

◆ Musician

There are days when I get out of bed and think, "Oh God, I can't face the flute!" But I have a way of coping with that. I give myself a month's vacation in August. I literally do not touch the flute. I've been known to lock it up in a bank vault.

*Stan Savant is the principal flutist for a regional symphony. He teaches flute at a nearby college and plays for weddings, parties, churches, and schools. These performances are sometimes solo and sometimes with other musicians.*

◆ ◆ ◆

I began playing the flute in the seventh grade. I caught on quickly to understanding rhythms and reading the notes, but mostly I practiced. It really wasn't anything to do with talent. I wasn't a better musician than any of the other players, but I could play the notes better because I had put in the time.

After high school I was offered an academic scholarship and a partial music scholarship at a university. I studied music education because I knew every musician should expect to teach — it's an economic necessity. After college, I learned about the job I have now from some friends who were playing in the symphony. I feel very lucky to have this job. It was a matter of my being in the right place at the right time. Today most orchestras — major, minor, and Podunk — announce positions in a paper called *International Musician*. You send in a résumé, maybe a tape, and if you're asked to audition, you go, at your own expense, and sit behind a screen with a small committee of orchestra personnel out front listening. The playing is totally anonymous. It's terrifying! One little foul-up and you're out. There are so many fine artists who cannot find jobs. Hundreds of people in the U.S. could do my job. But they can't find work. Many are waiting tables in New York or Los Angeles.

When I got my seat in the orchestra, I didn't really have any conception of what it was going to be like living on so little money. I was just out of school and new to town. I was determined not to take money from my parents, but I had to hide how bad things were from them. I was really unhappy because while I was playing well and doing what I wanted to do, the money angle was so bad that it crossed over into everything else. At times

I couldn't even afford to go to McDonald's. If it hadn't been for a few very nice people, I really think I would have just given up. Sometimes in symphonies there is a very cutthroat feeling, but we supported one another. We found things to do that didn't take money, like going to museums or walking through the old wealthy sections of town. Going out to eat was a big deal, a rarity. Those years taught me the value of money. In the world today, making a buck is a big deal, and if that's important to you, music is not the area to go into. If you want to be a musician, marry a doctor.

Maybe if it had been a little easier back then,

I wouldn't be as successful now. One of the things I had a lot of time for was practicing. I learned a lot. When I got out of college, I thought I was a good player, but suddenly I was in a situation where everyone played as well as me. I wasn't a star anymore. It really makes you work harder, and the hard work is more important than talent or creativity. Very few people are so talented that they don't have to work. For me, practicing was never a problem. Fear is a great motivator! There's an old saying: "If you skip one day, you can tell. If you skip two, the audience can tell." I think that's very true. Sometimes I spend seven or eight hours a day learning a new orchestra piece.

This job doesn't give me a lot of contact with others while I'm practicing, but the fulfillment of that practice is when I'm in the middle of a whole mass of people. We always perform *to* someone. There's an audience of generally fifteen hundred to two thousand people, and in a performance we need to give them something. They went to the trouble of coming. They got dressed up and bought a ticket. They are there! I always strive to give them the most I can.

Music should paint a picture in the audience's mind. Otherwise, these pieces are just a bunch of notes. The audience is not going to applaud because they thought, "He played that well." Hopefully, they are going to applaud because they had

some sort of vision. The audience's appreciation is so important. They give you energy that you want to turn around and give back to them. So it's important to make the music special, to make it reach out from where you are to the audience and touch them. Make it beautiful, intense, loud, fast, ugly. Whatever you think the music is saying. Once you reach yourself, you can begin to reach others. And it's the most wonderful, heartwarming feeling to finish a performance and hear the applause. It's exhilarating each time!

When the performances don't work, I sweat a

lot. My fingers sweat, my lips quiver, I can't breathe, I get saliva in my mouth. It's like everything collapses on itself and I become a little mass of quivering flesh trying to get through, trying to concentrate. And just when I think I've conquered nervousness, it comes back to haunt me. I can have the most simple thing that I am totally prepared for and suddenly some combination of factors happens and I literally vibrate and sweat and I can't breathe. There's no rhyme or reason. I just have to practice not thinking about it.

This country is not like Europe, where musicians and music teachers are idolized. But over the years I think I've proven something to myself about my work. I like to think that what I do, and what all artists do, is something so unique there's no one else who can imitate it exactly. You can hear the music of *Romeo and Juliet* a thousand times with the same player and yet, if the player wishes, each time there is something unique, something different. It may be only a very subtle difference — it's like snowflakes.

Uniformity is usually what is valued in many professions — the ability to come out with the same results. There are many musicians who try for uniformity, but to me they aren't musicians, they're technicians. Playing the flute gives me the chance to take the notes on the page — to take what somebody else gave me — and make it something personal, something special. The conductor can tell me what to play, how loud and how fast, but the interpretation of notes is one little personal thing that's mine. So every time I do my job, I have the chance to create something that hopefully other people will want to see or hear or feel. I create something that I hope will have meaning to somebody else.

I try not to be too comfortable in my job. The edge is necessary for performance. It's too easy to become complacent. I've been here many years. I'm settled in. But when I get on the stage and it's my turn to play, if I'm not ready, I know it. The audience may not know, but I know, and the people around me know. It only takes one bad performance to bring things back into focus, to make me remember why I'm there. I'm comfortable about performing, but I have to keep that edge. What I do is up for show. A musician performing is like an artist hanging up a piece on the wall. That is me. My life.

# RHONDA HALL

## ◆ Detective

I have learned to sort of get through the rap-sheet side of the person and the criminal side of them. I can look at the human factor in them all. As a patrol officer, I dealt mostly with the victims and the complainants. But in this job I have the opportunity to get closer to the criminal element. I get to know the person.

*After almost eight years as a patrol officer, Rhonda Hall became a police detective in the robbery division. Her job now involves investigating kidnapping, armed robberies, muggings, bank robberies, forgeries, and purse snatchings. Working closely with the patrol officers, she sets up and follows through on arrests, and she sometimes makes the arrests herself. She also spends a great deal of time testifying in court.*

◆　◆　◆

To be quite honest with you, being a police officer was a little bit more than what I had expected. I had always seen — and I think most people see — the glamour side of law enforcement on television. It looks so adventuresome and so glamorous, but when I'm really out there in the middle of it, I'm out there dealing with a human factor. These criminals and victims are not stars. They are not actors, but real people.

I think I was emotionally sort of ill-prepared for some of the things that I saw — like little kids accidentally shooting themselves to death. I have always been an optimist and was brought up to believe that there is hope for everyone, that everybody can be helped. But I have encountered transients, or mentally disturbed people, or homeless people, or poverty-stricken people where I knew truly in my heart, after exhausting every possible avenue I could to get these people some help, that for some people there really is no hope.

Basically, this is really a good job for a curious person, because, if you sit down and think about it, what are you doing out there? You are involving yourself in other people's business, be it burglary or domestic disturbance. It is a people-oriented job. If you don't like people, and you don't like dealing with people, this is not the job you ought to be in.

Believe it or not, I can develop some compassion for the criminals when I get to talking to them. I start looking at the rap sheet and all the bad things the person's been convicted of, and I sit down there talking to him and find it hard to believe that this person is really capable of doing all of this. I can actually say that I have run into hardened, hardened criminals who have beautiful personalities. They knew that I couldn't help them out, they were in jail and it was going to be up to a D.A. or a judge. Their destiny was in the D.A.'s or judge's hands, and they had nothing to gain by being nice to me. But they were. I found that to be shocking. To break any law is wrong. But there are some people I sit down and talk with and I can sort of understand what drove them to that point of desperation to steal or to rob somebody. I can understand — not condone, but understand.

Court cases can become almost like sporting

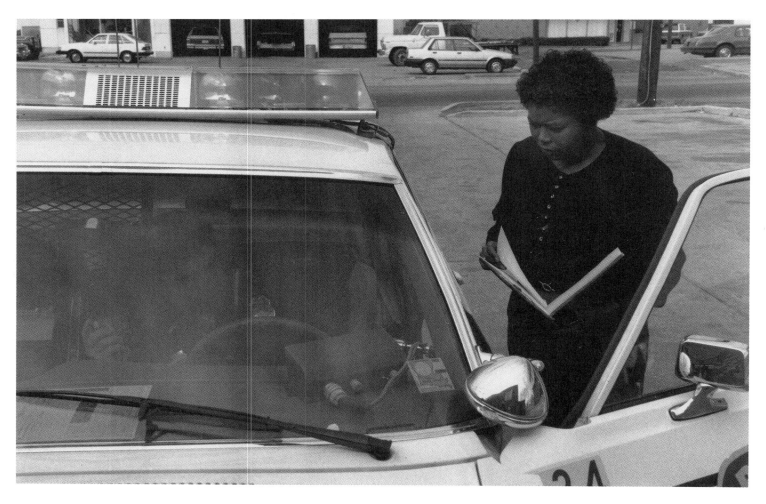

events — competitions. The defense attorney has his team members, and the prosecuting attorney has *his* team members. I am a team member for the prosecuting attorney. It's a good feeling when we win! When a suspect that I know is guilty is convicted, it makes me appreciate the method to the madness and it makes me see that my job is really, really worthwhile. So, one or two may walk. They may get smart enough lawyers to get them off. But by the same token, if I put three, four, five, or six behind bars, that's less crime in the street and it shows that my hard work has paid off.

But when I've worked real, real hard on a

case — when I've worked and worked to develop it and to put on the very best testimony and to bring forth the very best and strongest evidence that I could — and we lose it over some technicality, that makes me sick! I mean emotionally sick. It doesn't do any good to get mad. It's a learning experience. There are so many things that could make us lose the case — so many small things: the way we handled the evidence, where the evidence is stored, the chain of evidence which cannot be broken. It's those small things. Losing is a constant reminder that down the line we have

to do it right every time. So losing has its benefits, but it's hard. It's really hard.

As a detective, I have to be flexible — so flexible — because this is a job where the adrenaline is pumping like wild one minute and the next minute everything is calm and serene. I might have to leave the scene of a bank robbery and then go and study notebooks full of mug shots for hours. It's like going from an extreme high to an extreme low in a matter of minutes and the tension is always going to be difficult. I never know what the next call is going to be. I like that. It is un-

predictable and it makes work really, really exciting. There's no way we call a day a typical workday. There's never a typical workday.

I have sat down and started working on case folders at eight-thirty in the morning and stayed until five o'clock at night without leaving. And there are times when I may go out and be in the ditches looking for a suspect all day long. When we get information on a suspect, we have to get up and move right then. So I could be in a drainage ditch in the next ten minutes, or I could be on the top of a building in the next ten minutes, or under a house, or in a vacant warehouse with big rats running all around. We never depend on going home clean, the way we came to work.

# TOM STINSON

### ◆ Farmer

I don't think of farming as a job, because I like it. I think of a job as something that you have to do. I consider mine an occupation. I'm working for myself and I'm involved with nature and I see things that human hands can't make. We can't make a pecan. We can't make a cotton plant.

*Tom Stinson lives on the outskirts of a very small rural town near the land where three generations of his family have farmed. He and his brother grow mostly cotton on their farm, but they also harvest pecans from about eight hundred pecan trees and farm wheat, soybeans, and milo.*

◆ ◆ ◆

I think the thing about farming that you have to understand is that it can be very rewarding or very discouraging. What I like about it is that I'm working for myself and that I'm close to nature. I like the saying, "The man who plants a seed and waits believes in God." All we can do as human beings is physically put the seed in the ground. It takes God to warm the ground up by the sunshine.

To me the greatest feeling in the world is to go and plant the seed, get a rain, or whatever it takes to cause that seed to grow, and then go out there and see all those seeds up. I feel closer to God than most people ever can. You sit in a city and all you look at are brick walls and concrete. I am out in the open; sometimes, I am out in the cool morning before the sun comes up and I see a sunrise. I am able to witness the sunset — and who else does that at work? What other occupation really has that chance? We're able to see things from the beginning to the end.

The negative side to farming is that I can work real hard and end up with a poor crop and I lose money. In most production industries, production can be stopped or cut down when the product isn't selling. If automobile companies manufacture a car and it is not selling well, they will slow production down and let sales catch up. With farming, after the seed is planted, and after I have put $x$ number of dollars in it, I've pretty well got to carry it on through. We are committed to that crop until harvest, no matter what the weather does, no matter what the price does, and no matter how that plant produces.

It requires more and more money to farm. Thirty or forty years ago, if a farmer had a poor crop, say on a farm this size, he might lose ten or fifteen thousand dollars. Now, he might lose two or three hundred thousand. So one year can wipe him out, where several years ago he could come back. Farming requires borrowing a lot of money and then a lot of effort to pay it back.

As times get hard and I see people quitting or

I read all this bad publicity that the farmers are getting, I think, what would I do if we have a bad crop or we lost money? I know that it would be hard for me at this time to, first off, find a job, and second, to work for somebody else when I've worked for myself for so long.

Several years ago I had some trouble with the cotton picker, and I was up under it and oil was dripping down on me. It was real cold and had been raining. It was noon, and I said, "You know, people in town are sitting back eating lunch now." And I said, "Here I am under this dang cotton picker, oily and dirty and cold." I said, "Man, I don't know about this life." Then I

nature — I really enjoy that part of it. I see the leaves come out on the pecan trees, then the blooms come out. The female bloom and then the male bloom comes out, and the wind blows and pollinates the female bloom, and then you see a pecan come on. So I am involved with the whole process.

Another thing I like about farming is that it's not the same thing day after day after day. You take a man who is working at the factory, his job never changes. But with us, it changes daily. We very seldom see the same thing. We may be involved in the same process of farming, but there's something new every day. Then those processes change. You plant, you cultivate, you irrigate, and you harvest. That keeps it from being boring.

Workdays on a farm are a lot longer than workdays on a regular job. During the summer, we are cultivating and irrigating and I might be out there at midnight and then be back there at six o'clock in the morning. In the fall, harvest is also a tough time, because we work twelve or fourteen hours a day. After we've finished harvesting, when we are completely through, we start preparing the land again at the end of the year and work through January and February. April is when we really start planting and getting busy again.

thought later on, "Well, I'm working for myself and most of them are working for somebody else." That's the biggest reward, I think.

Then there is being close to God and watching

I feel I was lucky to be able to start farming — to have an uncle that left me some of the land and some of the equipment to get started. I also feel like I've stayed informed, and I continue to stay informed and keep up and do a better job each year. I've never been satisfied with my production. In 1964, if I made a bale per acre, I really had a good crop. Now I want to make two bales per acre. I'm now making a bale and a half to a bale and three-quarters. So I've never been satisfied with what I make. I don't know if that's good or bad. But it doesn't mean I won't go broke tomorrow. I understand that part of it. Because all I can do is the best I can. I've had to come to grips with this personally. I do the best I can do, and I work hard, and if I don't make it . . . I don't make it.

# CHRISTIE WALTON

### ◆ Television Journalist

Newscasts are unforgiving. They fall at given times every day and there has to be someone here to put them together. Just because it's a slow Thursday night, we can't say, "No news! See you around; we're not going to do it." Someone has to be here and fill that half hour's time slot with something.

24

*Christie Walton was a television reporter for several years, specializing in feature stories rather than hard news. She still does some reporting on weekdays, but the main part of her job now involves anchoring (presenting most of the news on camera), producing (writing the news and deciding what goes where), and being assignment editor (deciding what stories need to be covered) for the Saturday and Sunday newscasts.*

◆　◆　◆

The term *journalist* refers loosely to the act of going out, finding out about something, and then communicating that information to someone else. Involved in that are an awful lot of decisions: Is it important? Why is it important? Why should the viewer care? We want to do the essence of the story, the "Who? What? Where? When? Why?," but we also need to consider the viewers. How does this story affect their lives? *Does* it affect their lives? Why should Joe Six-Pack, John Doe out there, care about the story? That has a lot to do with whether we'll cover a story.

Some people would call what I do for a living "being nosy" or "digging in somebody else's business" or being a kind of vulture. And in a strange sense, that may be true. We're waiting for something to go wrong so we can make a story out of it. But at the same time, if we are uncovering or doing a story about a public official who is steal-

ing money, there is a public interest in that, because it's not just that official who's affected. It's all of the people who pay the taxes.

But there are parts of this job that don't suit my personality — the part where I have to make people angry. People sometimes have to be asked "the hard question," the question I know they aren't going to want to hear. And they aren't going to like me because I've asked it. Very often I will go into a situation that is not pleasant, and that is one of the reasons that I don't do very much hard news. I prefer to do feature stories.

But in some instances, the importance of that hard question overrides my desire to be liked. In the instance of a recent story on allegations of child abuse, my interest in that — the belief that maybe there is a wrong here — made it easier for me to ask tough questions. I hoped the person that I asked respected the fact that I was only doing my job.

One of the best things about this job is that when I walk in the door each day I don't know what I'm going to be doing. It's something different every day. Some days I may sit at my desk and make phone calls and get information and never leave the building. I like anchoring an awful lot, but I think my favorite part of the job is meeting the people — going out and never knowing who I'm going to meet. I meet regular people on the street who tell me their opinion of something on the news. I've met rock stars like Brian Adams. I've had a chance to meet senators and develop friendships with congressmen, because I cover them a lot. I've met a whole spectrum of people. I've met people who are so off the wall you wouldn't believe it, and people who are so incredibly intelligent that they make you feel like the most ignorant slime in the world!

My least favorite part of the job is the deadlines. The time! The highest pressure is making that deadline. It's getting the best information I can, the best picture I can, getting them laid down and edited in time. The pressure is frustrating, but it's

a piece of the job. I work within the time constraints, because no one is going to say, "Oh, we'll put off the six o'clock news and wait for your story to be finished." I learned that when I need to work quickly, I work quickly. And I do the work without ignoring facts or details and without losing those basic premises that we work on:

the "Who? What? When? Where? and Why?". And I try to show it in a compelling way.

I may do an hour interview and still not think I've gotten what I needed. I may have to pull fifteen, twenty seconds out of that. So I make choices. I'm a gatekeeper for this information in a lot of ways. I decide what to let the interviewed

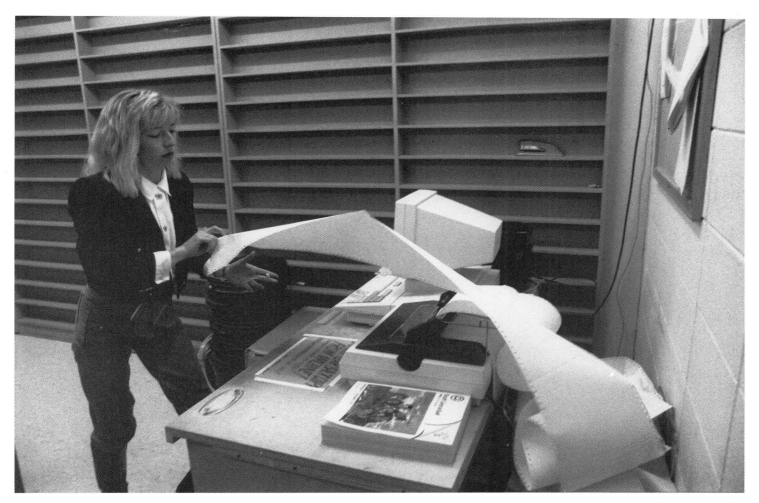

subject say and what I can say. I choose what we call "sound bites" — snippets of a conversation from an interview — to impart some information. I hope that ten or fifteen seconds says something. Amazingly enough, a lot can be said in that amount of time.

I suppose my job is like any other. Not every day is going to be the big story — there is a lot of boredom that goes along with the job. But some days, it's exciting to get to work because I know I'll be working on something that I've really gotten excited about, something I really want to tell people about. The best news stories are the ones that are told in the way that you would walk up

to a friend and say, "Can you believe what happened today? You should see!" That's the excitement of this business, because it has become the "back fence" of our society. It's the talking. It's a personal form of communication, and that's

exciting to me — that intimacy that television brings.

When I'm on the air, I'm in people's bedrooms, in their kitchens, in their cars — I'm in a lot of aspects of people's lives! Very intimate! That's scary at times, because people know me and know a lot about me, and I've never seen them. And they feel a connection with me, personally. They feel like they own a little piece of me sometimes. I have lost an aspect of anonymity. What I do is very much under scrutiny by the people around me.

I will go to the grocery store in my oldest sweat suit and tennis shoes, and someone will see me and go, "Well, golly! You don't look like that on TV!" I'm used to it and I laugh with them. I say, "Yeah, the makeup does a great job, doesn't it!"

# CARL E. STEWART

### ◆ Judge

Most people are in court because they believe they have an issue and they want their fair shake. The last thing I want people to feel is that they are not getting a fair shake. I don't ever want a person to leave my courtroom feeling "I don't even think he was listening when I was testifying. I don't think that once he heard me talking" — because he has a drawl or a twang or didn't speak good English or is rural or urban, or rich or poor, or whatever.

*Carl E. Stewart is a state district court judge elected to a six-year term. He began his legal career as a military lawyer for the Army. Afterward, he was a public service lawyer for the government, and then he briefly pursued a private practice. Now, as a judge, he decides both civil and criminal questions. The civil issues primarily involve disputes over money, property, and domestic mat-* *ters, and the criminal issues range from traffic violations to murder.*

◆   ◆   ◆

In the early sixties, when I was growing up, many of the social changes that came about were the result of lawyers who took actions to have leg-

islation passed, such as the Voting Rights Act and anti-discrimination laws. I saw lawyers as advocates trying to bring a whole class of society into the mainstream of society. I saw how lawyering, how a lawsuit against the establishment, could be used as a tool to bring about change.

At fourteen, fifteen, and sixteen years old I was keenly aware of the great upheavals of social change occurring. I mean, I lived in the midst of that! And I could identify with those who were seeking to bring about change through the court system. That's what I liked — as opposed to trying to bring about change through violence or some other way.

Another reason why I wanted to become a lawyer is that lawyering is a people occupation, and I've always been people-oriented. I majored in psychology in college because I liked trying to discover what made people do what they do. Lawyers, to me, engage in psychology all the time in trying not only to figure out what people do but also to change their behavior. This fascinated me because it fit my own desire to work with people and try to understand and modify their behavior.

I liked trial work and the adversarial nature of being in a courtroom arena. I loved it! It got me in the arena against an able opponent. But I always wanted to be that third-party person who got to make the decisions after having heard two or more lawyers present their cases persuasively and powerfully. I wanted to make that next step and be that third party who got to make the de-

cision. I like dispute resolution. I like being in the throes of having to make tough decisions and having to weigh and balance evidence and considerations of fairness.

The fascinating thing about being a judge is that I'm not dealing with a Hollywood script — there's no predetermined ending. We're talking about real live people who have real bona-fide differences of opinion. Whether the disputes re-

late to who gets the child, or whether somebody has to pay damages for a claim. Or whether somebody is locked up for the rest of their life. Or whether somebody is released from jail and goes home because there is not enough evidence to hold them. They're real live issues that come out of everyday situations. I deal up-close and in-person with the issues that people read about in the newspaper.

Not all cases involve big, thorny, supercomplicated, mind-boggling issues. It's just that somebody's got to make a decision, and the people in front of me haven't been able to do it. That's when I get a great sense of satisfaction. Not that I have come down with some earthshaking ruling, but the fact that two sets of people now have a decision made for them from which they can govern their lives. That's a service that, as a judge, I provide. They know that "there is somebody who will tell us what to do." And once I decide, they go on and they're happy.

The decision-making process itself is quite lonely because it is, by nature, a solitary process. If one side is weighted far greater than the other side, then the questions that need answering are pretty easy. But when the sides are relatively equal, then the questions can be tough. There is

maintains as much touch with the realities of everyday experiences as possible. Because when I am sitting alone in my chambers reading over the

no way I can plug these factors into the magic of technology — computers — and get a readout that says, "Well, this is what you do." Judging is still very much a human process, and hopefully when a person is a judge, the person is as well-rounded as possible, as well-read as possible, and volumes of material and the sides of a case seem pretty equal, all I have to help me decide is the sum total of my life experiences, my common sense, and my sense of what's just and right.

I like being in the position to make that decision. I like being in the position to balance those interests, to make that call. I like the challenge of weighing those close situations and of having to bring to bear all my life's experiences, my sense of right and wrong, my sense of what justice is. To me, that's the essence, the ultimate opportunity for my sense of right and wrong to manifest itself. Nobody else can do that but me. I don't have a conference with three people. We don't take a vote. It comes down to me and my own sense of being in balance, my being in tune with what's just and right.

Some would run away from deciding tough cases and say, "Hey, I don't want to make that kind of call. I wouldn't want to have somebody's fate in my hands. I wouldn't want to decide whether the mother or the father gets the child in that divorce case. I wouldn't want to decide whether somebody gets ten years or forty years." Many people, even many lawyers, would not want to make those decisions for very good reasons. But despite the fact that it's hard and I anguish over it, and sometimes I wonder whether I have made the right decision, I never wish that someone else had to make the decision.

# ELLEN WEILAND

### ◆ Computer Programmer

We deal with the bugs in the system, the problems. Many of the hours in our day are spent in what we call "fighting fires" — figuring out why a terminal isn't working. And that's kind of fun. It really is. In some ways it's like being a doctor. He has someone that's sick. We have a terminal that's sick, or a program that's sick. And we have to try to figure out what the problem is and how to fix it.

*Ellen Weiland has worked eight years in City Hall as a systems programmer. She helps set up and run the large computers that keep the many city services operating smoothly.*

◆　◆　◆

In college, I started taking a couple of computer courses and just fell in love with working with computers. People think that you have to be strong in math to be in computers, but it's not really true. You don't use bare math; you use the logic part of math, and that's what you need for computer sciences: logical thinking and logical processes.

After I got my degree in computer science, I moved here and went to work for the city. At the time, they were beginning a conversion from one

Without it, the terminals and printers won't work. It's kind of like the brain of the system.

It was really exciting in the beginning because it was almost like building my own little baby. I created the system almost from the ground level all the way up. And it's still there! I took a piece of hardware that did nothing and started putting software on it to make it start doing something productive. It's changed quite a bit. When I came, we had one machine. Now we have four different machines.

We are a city-support service. If the machine is not running properly, then the police have trouble

machine to a newer machine. Their systems programmer had left and they pulled me in there to work on the new machine. The "machine," the central processing unit, is the heart of the system.

dispatching policemen to crimes. Or the fire people have trouble dispatching their trucks to a fire. Or the cashiers in the revenue section have trouble taking cash from a customer coming in to pay a bill. We support the accounting division that pays all the bills for the city and writes all the checks. We support the city court system. We support the payroll and personnel system which actually pays the city's thirty-five hundred employees.

We have all the information for everybody in City Hall. All the individual programs and functions work on my machine. I have to make sure they are all working properly. If there is a bug in the water-billing system, I identify it as being in that program and then either I fix it or I find another person who can. But if a part of the structure has fallen, I have to rebuild that section. It is a support system, a kind of framework. We don't wallpaper the wall, but we actually put the wall there so that somebody can wallpaper or paint it or do whatever they want to do to it.

As we add people using the machines, we have to add more storage room for the information and we have to connect all the users. It's kind of like a highway system. All the traffic is going down one lane and we keep putting more and more information in, and there's more and more traffic. And soon, the system is just like the highways in a big city — the information flow stops because there's too much traffic. The system backs up. So we have to redesign the system so that access to the information is faster.

I do feel I am affecting the people of this city. When a fire dispatcher calls me and says, "Look, we're just not getting a good response!" I think, "Well, these guys need to get fire trucks out to these fires." I even feel this way when working with a cashier, which is not as critical. But we've all been in a cashier line and had to wait and wait and wait. And then we get up there and they say, "Well, my computer is down. I can't do anything!" That's frustrating. I want to try to get the machine that is doing that function to work much better so that people don't get frustrated, and so

that we can get our fire trucks to the fires.

The more I get into my work, the more I realize how much there is to learn. It's like there's this endless pit of things to learn. Sometimes it's discouraging learning more and more and seeing that there is so much more to learn. But it's exciting too! I know that I am never going to come to a point where I know it all. If I get to that point, I might as well move on somewhere else. I need to keep growing, to keep learning, and that's what's exciting about my job.

The machine can frustrate me sometimes, especially if I have just gotten into something new and I don't totally understand it yet. If I do something really simple and it just doesn't work, I think, "Well, what happened? Why isn't it working?" That can be very frustrating until I finally figure it out, until I read something or talk to somebody that explains this kind of black hole that I didn't see before. And if a machine goes down for some reason, or even part of it is not functioning, then the pressure can be really heavy from management: "We need this machine up — *now!*" And that can be frustrating. It can be stressful.

My job is indirectly helping people. I'm not usually right there face-to-face with people trying to help them, but the things that I do are helping them do their job. I work mostly with the machine, but I like working with people. I guess I don't work with people as much as I would in another job, but I work with the things that they work with — making a machine that helps them do their job.

I love my job! It allows me some creativity — it's creating something. I can take something that is just sitting there doing nothing and actually make it do something productive and then keep it running productively. It's one little box and I'm one person, but I'm helping six or seven hundred people, or even more when you consider that the information is shared among all kinds of people outside of City Hall.

# ELIAS SIFUENTES

## ♦ Restaurateur

> I do it all. I open the restaurant in the morning and I close it up at the end of each day. From the minute that I open the door I do everything that has to be done until I close the door. There are a thousand things that have to be done in a restaurant.

*Elias Sifuentes has run a Mexican restaurant for almost ten years. After having other jobs and working part-time in Mexican restaurants for many years, he and a friend decided to start their own.*

♦ ♦ ♦

I used to work at a General Electric factory. I was a punch-press operator. I was making good money, but working there frustrated me because I like to work with people, talk to people. And there, there was nobody to talk to. The only time I got together with others was during lunch or during meetings. And I said to myself, "I like the money. I like the benefits. But this is not what I want to do all my life."

I've worked part-time in Mexican restaurants for most of my life being a waiter, cook, dishwasher. Not because I was hungry for money, but because I told myself, "Someday I'm going to do something for myself and I want to learn the

to pay our bills. I told him, "That's what it is. That's the way it goes. I like to have a payday, but we just can't do it right now." When we expanded the place, we got more customers, more business. We felt better because it finally started to pay off. We were very pleased. We saw more traffic and we started putting money in our pockets. We felt better. One hundred percent. The success has continued ever since.

In the beginning I was kind of shaky and afraid because I knew very little spoken English. I could more or less write in English. And to learn all the

whole trade." While I was at GE, the restaurant where I was working part-time was closed down. So my partner and I got together, and I said, "What are you going to do?" He said, "I don't know." I said, "Let's get a place of our own! I'll do the cooking. You be the front man. What else do we need?" He liked the idea, and so we put the idea to work, and it works.

We started from scratch. In the beginning, we didn't get a paycheck. The only money we got was to buy groceries. My partner was kind of frustrated. Whatever we were making was going trade — that's a big step. In Mexico I took a year of business administration in college, so I had my year's training. It's not a whole lot, but it helped me when I needed it. I learned about supervising, expenses, administration. How to buy, how to spend, how to control, all these kinds of things.

But now I am learning on the job. I believe you learn a lot better when you exercise what you are doing. To me, I have no other choice but to learn — be forced to learn to do the job. Until now, I have been fortunate to do a good job. There are a good number of people depending on me, and I haven't let them down yet. My twenty-eight employees depend on me to be smart enough to continue the business for all of us — so all of us can make a good living. A lot of places come and go. Even big companies with big money and good managers — they are gone. Fortunately we have managed to stay.

To stay in business, I have to be aggressive. I have to fight. If I go by another Mexican restaurant and I see a line of people, I say to myself, "They are doing something right." If I go to my place and see nobody there, I say, "I am doing something wrong." So then I have to do something different. I must be more conscious of my customers and give them more attention. That's what I do best — pay attention to my customers. Talk to them. Meet them. Let them know who I am.

When customers complain, they keep me more

aware. They open my eyes. I don't mind having a complaint once in a while. Nobody likes to have those, but if I do, I want to be sure that the same customer doesn't have the same complaint twice. I feel bad when a customer comes and tells me that he waited too long and never got service. I feel bad when a customer comes to tell me that a waiter has been rude. When a customer tells me that the food doesn't have enough seasoning, I feel bad. But I face the customer. It doesn't matter what happens, they always come to me. They say they want to see me. I say, "Fine, no problem."

I take all kinds of complaints, which can get me down a lot.

I usually come to work at eight o'clock in the morning. Normally, I stay until two o'clock in the afternoon, doing the supervising, the purchasing, seeing the salesmen, seeing the advertisers. Then I go to my house to take a shower, and I come back at five o'clock. I stay until closing time at ten o'clock. We usually leave the place at eleven or twelve, after cleaning up.

When customers walk in my door, I receive them in the friendliest way I can. I see to it that they get service properly from my busboy, from my waitress, even from myself. If anything takes longer than it's supposed to, that is what I am there for — to take care of that kind of problem. Afterward, when the customer is finished, I come to the table again — maybe two, three more times. "Is everything OK? Everything satisfactory?" That's my job in the front of the restaurant. Then back in the kitchen, I see that everything comes out properly. I do that myself every morning. I taste everything, believe me! Chips, hot sauce, dressing, beans, Spanish rice, cheese sauce, you name it. I taste everything to see it is prepared right, before we open the doors. That keeps me going through lunchtime. Sometimes we stay so busy that I forget to sit down and have a meal.

A man who had come up from Mexico asked me the other day about opening a restaurant. He

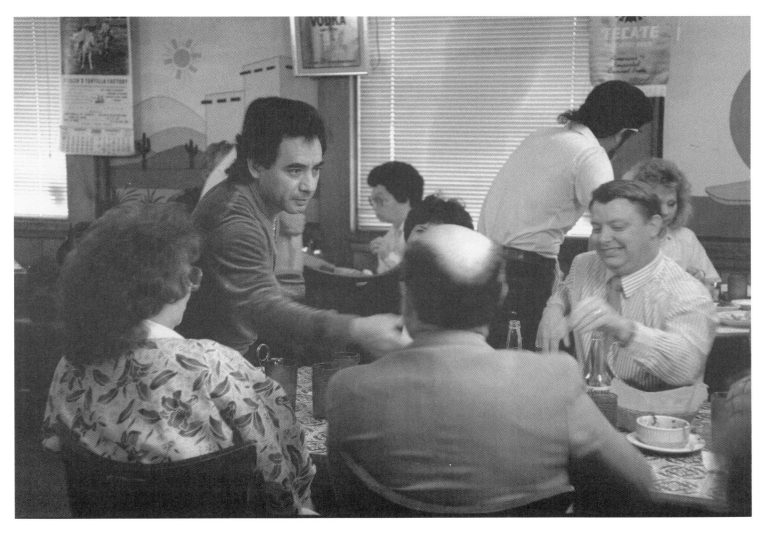

said to me, "If you did it, I can do it." I said, "Yes, you can do it." Then he said, "You tell me how." I said, "Wait a minute. You just told me you can do it. You don't need my advice. You can do it! But if you don't have your heart in it, forget it."

# JEAN JOHNSON

## ◆ Social Worker

> God gives me health and strength as I work from paycheck to paycheck, and I'm giving something back. There are a lot of people out there less fortunate than I am. I used to worry about being broke, but then I found out that other people out there have nothing. Absolutely nothing. If I can do something to brighten their day, I am thankful.

*Jean Johnson worked for a federal social-service agency for a short time but left when she tired of the office work. Now she works for a social-service agency associated with the Catholic church that receives its funding entirely from donations. Her job puts her directly in touch with people suffering from poverty, hunger, and domestic violence.*

◆   ◆   ◆

Our agency's primary responsibilities are to assist people in paying their utilities and rent and to provide shelter. Now, since I've been here, I go a

little bit beyond that. I go out and make home visits to families calling us for assistance. I make home visits to see how much they need. A lot of times I go out and find more than just their unpaid utility bills. Like yesterday, I went to see this lady

who wanted someone to pay her rent. When I got to the house, the only furniture that she had was two chairs. She had five children sleeping on the floor. She didn't even have a stove. So I will try to find the necessary furniture for that home.

Doing social work, you really get out there and actually do the job. Every day is something different. It's always exciting to me. Every day you have a different problem. It's a challenge. Someone may come to me and say, "Jean, I have a family with five kids and no place to stay." Right now, emergency housing for homeless families is very limited. It's a challenge to go out there and try to find something before five o'clock for this family so they can have a place to sleep and some food and clothing.

I try to be a problem-solver — whatever the need might be. If it's going to the police department, going to the judge or some type of city official, I will go. If a family needs furniture, and if we don't have the furniture, and if the Salvation Army doesn't have the furniture, I will call around to different stores and explain the problem: "Hey, I need such-and-such for this family." Welfare department, the same thing: "We need such-and-such a thing." Child protection: "What can be done for these children?" I start at the bottom and go to the top to get the job done.

I don't know where to go in all cases. At times I just pick up the phone and make a few phone

53

calls. "I need some suggestions on this." I may call a minister: "Can you give me some advice on how to deal with this particular case?" I use all people to try to solve a problem. It might take fifteen people, but I call those people and try to get the job done if I can't do it myself.

I have seen it all in this job. Kids on drugs and alcohol. People fighting on the streets. I have seen I don't know how many people shot. I have seen ladies actually being mugged. I've even gotten hit upside the head by a lady. I had to go to the hospital. I thought about pressing charges against her. But I said, this is really not going to solve anything. There are other people out there who will appreciate me. Other people that need my assistance, so I don't give up.

I see that I make a difference, even if it might just be a temporary thing. I'm working now with a mother who has nine children. I visit the house and the house is really sort of like the city dump and a hog pen all at once. So I went into the home, and I assigned all the children different chores to do. The oldest child was fifteen, and I know I was putting a hell of a responsibility on her because the mother was out on the street somewhere. So the kids did clean up, and I rewarded

them with ice cream. I talked to them, hugged them, got the kids enrolled in school. I explained to them that times are really hard right now. I find that a lot of kids just need someone to love them.

After I worked with a crazy lady, a friend at the office said, "Jean, that lady really doesn't ap-preciate you doing this." But I feel that some-where down the line it's going to click in her head. I feel that. And working with those kids — those kids feel that, "Hey! Someone cares!" If I can help just one child out of those nine, I think I'll be doing good. Just one. And all the people I come

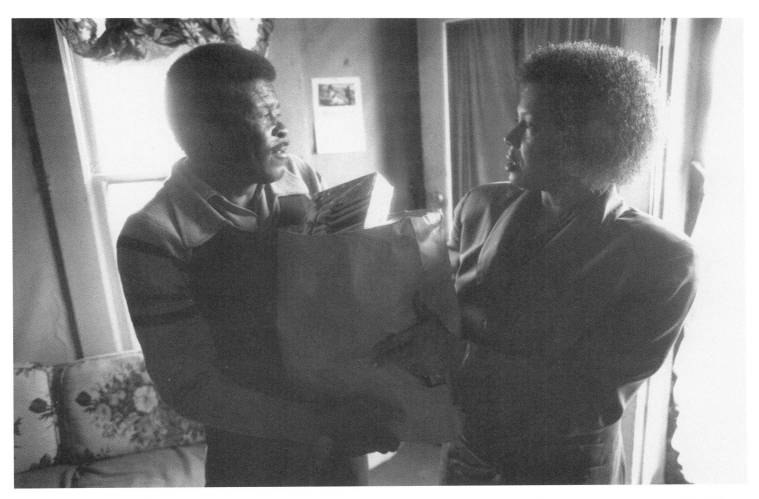

in contact with today, if I can help one, I'm doing fine. Paying someone's utility bills or finding them a place to stay or giving them some food. We were put here on this earth to help one another. I strongly believe that. I'm not saying I'm the best Christian in the world, because I have my faults just like everyone else, but I try to give something,

give myself. By me helping, I give myself. Wherever the needs, I try to do the damnedest to get the job done. Even if it's just for a moment — to bring some type of relief.

People ask me, "Jean, why do you do it?" I love what I'm doing, because I love being around people! No matter who they are and what they are — I love helping people. I get enjoyment out of it. I feel that I'm making somebody happy, even if they don't appreciate it at that particular time. I can say, "Hey, I did my part!" I don't look for any type of medal. I just go on and do it. I feel that I'm doing something that God wants me to do. Every day I ask Him to help me put a smile on someone's face because there's a lot of need.

I got a family some food and a place to stay at one of the agency houses. When I got to work Monday morning, the kids had left me some fruit on my desk and some fresh flowers. That made

my day. It's not the big things. It's the little things that count with me.

Some days I might not feel like going to work. But I say, "Hey, I'm going to miss something this day. Something exciting might happen this day that I can be a part of."

# JEFF FRANKLIN

### ✦ Air Force Pilot

There are some people that never lose their passion for flying. All they want to do is just get up away from the ground and fly. There's nothing wrong with that, but the Air Force is not the place to do it. Because the Air Force expects you to be something more than that.

*Jeff Franklin is a KC-10 pilot for the United States Air Force. The KC-10 is a cargo aircraft that refuels other Air Force aircraft in-flight. His job also includes evaluating the training of new KC-10 aircraft commanders, who then become totally responsible for the aircraft and its missions.*

◆　◆　◆

Since I was five or six years old, I've been very much oriented toward flying. My father had been a pilot in the Army. There was a period of time when he was out of the service flying fire patrol in light airplanes in northern Idaho where we lived. I flew with him almost every day then.

I expected the Air Force Academy to be one of the most trying times of my life, and it was. I went into the Academy and I was cut off. Very much cut off. I was there to survive on my own merits, whatever I could come up with inside myself. I didn't even see a telephone for six months. The Academy was so important to me because at eighteen years of age, I had to stand up on my own two feet and either make it or not make it.

Right after I graduated, the Air Force sent me through pilot training in Oklahoma. That lasted an entire year. It was an intense period of time. Pilot training is more concentrated than any other flying school you can go through. Civilians take three or four years to get the same qualifications

that I got in one year. All we did for a whole year was fly aircraft and go through the courses.

Right now my job is Director of KC-10 Training. It is my responsibility to teach the new pilots how to fly the KC-10's. These pilots come to me

right out of training and have no qualifications in a specific airplane in the Air Force. It used to be that the pilots came in and they pretty much flew everything — back in the Chuck Yeager days and all that. But because of the cost of training and the highly specialized nature of most of the airplanes, the Air Force can't afford to do that anymore. There is just too much difference between the airplanes. So, the airplane that a pilot signs on with when he comes through the door is the one that he is going to fly and be a specialist in for most of his career.

The KC-10 is an advanced tanker cargo aircraft. It is used for refueling fighters and whatever airplanes need fuel in flight. I can carry one hundred thousand pounds of cargo in the back. The KC-10 is used to deploy cargo to foreign locations — to Europe or wherever — all in one load. I can pull into a base that has fighters or whatever and load up all the support people and their equipment and their spare parts and then refuel the fighters on my wings all the way across the ocean. The idea is to be able to move a unit more easily. So the role that I have is worldwide strategic refueling — long-range refueling.

I have been all the way around the world in this airplane — the Far East, Australia. I've been to Japan four or five times. I've been to Europe probably fifteen or twenty times. I've been to the Middle East three or four times. Sometimes I may

stay there just overnight. Sometimes I may spend a week there. The travel is most definitely one of the advantages of my job. Sometimes it is hard to grasp where you really are, that you are, in fact, in Germany or in Australia or in Japan because the jet gets us there in such a short period of time. It's kind of neat to look at a picture of Stonehenge or Mount Aetna or Rome and be able to say, "Yeah! That's really how it looks. I was right there!" That was one of the reasons why I came in — to see the world.

Our missions can last fourteen or fifteen hours sometimes. That is fatiguing! There is a constant monitoring of all of the gauges and the airspeed and the altitude and the navigation. And when you start compounding that over a fourteen- or fifteen-hour flight, it becomes tremendously fatiguing. It was interesting to me that just sitting could be so tiring. Usually, there are two or three hours of postflight activity. I make sure that the maintenance personnel have gotten the airplane inspected and put fuel back on it for the next flight. I'm responsible for getting rooms for my crew. There is a significant number of reports that have to be sent back to the home unit — paperwork. So a fifteen-hour flight might very well be a twenty-three-hour day.

When I was on the crew and just responsible for flying aircraft, I really enjoyed it. I enjoyed all the aspects. I enjoyed going to places. I enjoyed flying, even though there were adverse hours sometimes and even though I couldn't look two weeks ahead and know what I was going to be doing. I got used to that. That's not a real big thing. In a lot of ways, the dynamic nature of the travel and hours kept me interested. But after about two thousand hours of flying time, after about five years or so, to me there had to be something more there than just pushing the throttles.

In the Air Force, you have to blossom. You have to show progression as a leader and an officer and as a pilot to move up through the system. The Air Force expects you to be something more than just a pilot. They need you to be their leaders

and their managers and to do all of the specialized things that it takes to make the flying mission work.

I am part of the Air Force for another reason: patriotism. I believe in military service. I can't walk away from service to my country at this point. That's kind of corny and that's kind of an old-fashioned idea these days, but I'm very patriotic about those things. Somebody has to do this. The country cannot survive without a standing military force. I'm part of that. And, as such, I'm supporting this nation.

There is a lot of pride involved in flying an airplane. Some people say, "Well, flying is a skill, but it's no more or less of a skill than driving a car." But there are certain things — reflexes — that go into the flying because you are moving in three axes and because it really isn't a natural thing. And with flying, everything's different every time. Every cloud deck is shaped just a little different. The winds are never the same twice.

You have to develop judgment, aviation judgment, and that is a difficult thing to even put a finger on. We're taking a machine that is capable of flight and we are operating it in an element that is not really our normal element. It's kind of magical all in itself. I'll go up there — especially at night this happens — and I'll be flying over the top of some big city looking down on a clear night with the stars and I'll say to myself, "I really can't believe the Air Force is paying me to do this!"

# CHARLOTTE KNOLL

## ◆ Nurse

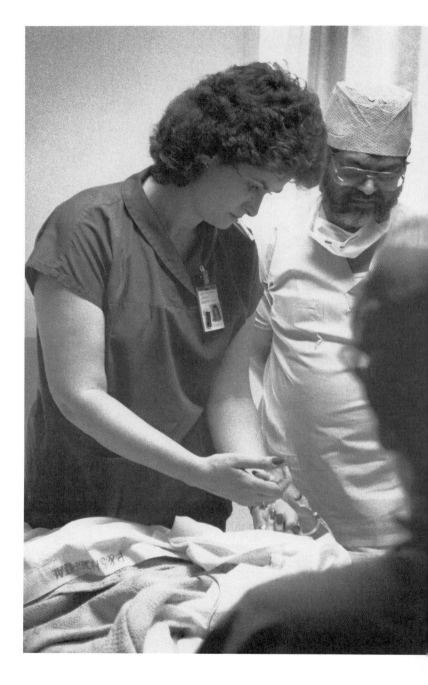

When we get a "Code Blue" — when a person's heart has stopped or they are not breathing — I go through the life-saving processes. If I save the person, a week or two later they will come by on their way out. Then I get this sense of power that makes me think, this is what I'm here for! It's hard to describe. It makes me feel great to know I had a part in saving this person's life.

*Charlotte Knoll is a registered nurse in charge of the emergency care center of a hospital. Her work involves making daily life-and-death decisions and training the other nurses working with her in the emergency room.*

◆ ◆ ◆

During summers and weekends, from the time I was fourteen years old, I helped work in the nursing home where my mom was a nurse. Patients in nursing homes are long-term. When you work in

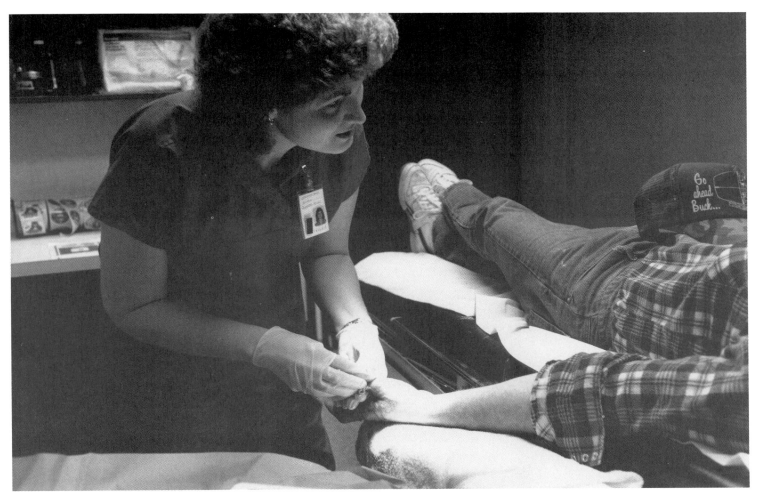

a nursing home, you are there with them for weeks, months, and years. I knew these people for years. I watched them get worse, and I watched them die. I went through a grieving process because I became attached to them. In a hospital, the patients are cared for, but it is only weeks or, at the most, months that they are here.

The nursing-home experience matured me. It taught me that caring was important and not to look at the bad — that the patients were going to die — but to do what I could to make them more comfortable or make their lives happier. I became almost like a family member to them, because they didn't have family who saw them every day.

Nursing to me is hands-on — being able not just to tell someone what needs to be done, but to actually perform the actions myself. I want to be the one to start the I.V. to save the patient's life. I want to be the one to shock the patient's heart if it has stopped. I want to be right in there with it. That's important to me. I can't imagine nursing and not doing that.

Maybe it's the excitement that I thrive on. I don't know why I feed on it. I guess that's why I'm in the emergency room. It makes my adrenaline flow. It makes me feel that time is important,

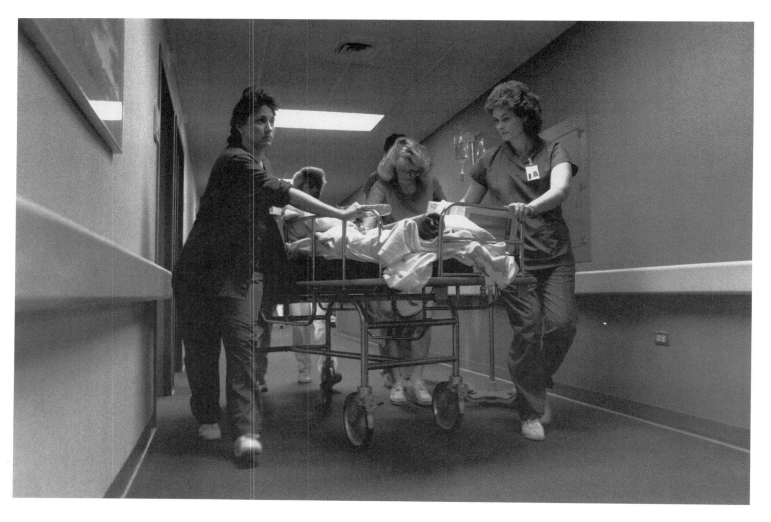

that I've got to make a decision! And it's up to me! Maybe it was good that I had the nursing-home experience, because I learned that's not all that I ever wanted to do — give baths, feed the patients, give medication. I needed more than that.

I thrive on critical situations. I love the feeling of knowing that when something happens, I've got to know what to do and I've got to do it whether there is anybody else around or not. It's just automatic. The more I do it, the better I feel about it. And when I'm through, I stand back and

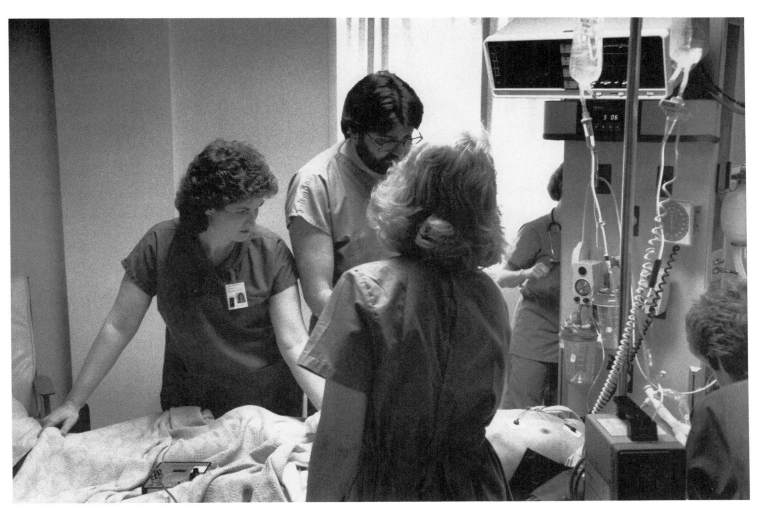

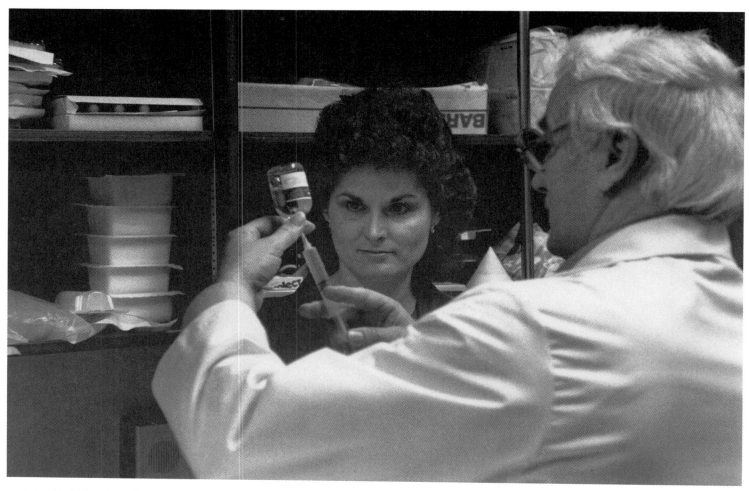

think, "If I hadn't been there . . ." I have this sense of power! Knowing that I've done it right and this person wouldn't be here talking to me if it hadn't been for what I did.

Starting out, the responsibilities were kind of scary — actually being out there by myself. In school, I did a lot of the same things I do here, but I always knew there was someone beside me or someone looking over my shoulder or someone stopping me before I did something wrong. But after I graduated, I had no one to ask. It was just me. In delivering a baby, no matter how much the book told me, no matter how much I had watched the process, it wasn't the same as actually touching it and knowing what I was doing. So I was always wondering, "Am I really doing this right?"

No matter how minor or how serious the situation with a patient, at some point what I do affects life or death. Whether I give the right medication, or too much of it, or not enough. There are so many factors involved. And it's not only what I do that's important, but also what I don't do.

The common emergencies are cuts at any age, from children on up, and falls that could involve cuts or breaks of any bone. We get a lot of falls with older people. A lot of industrial accidents, eye injuries — a person is working and gets some-

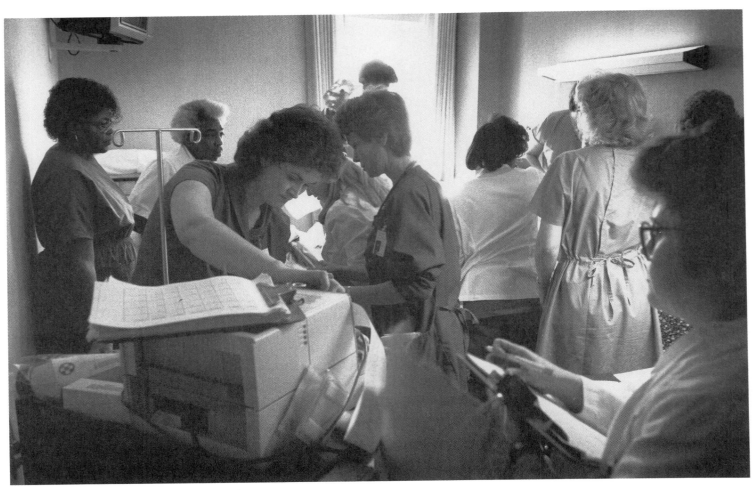

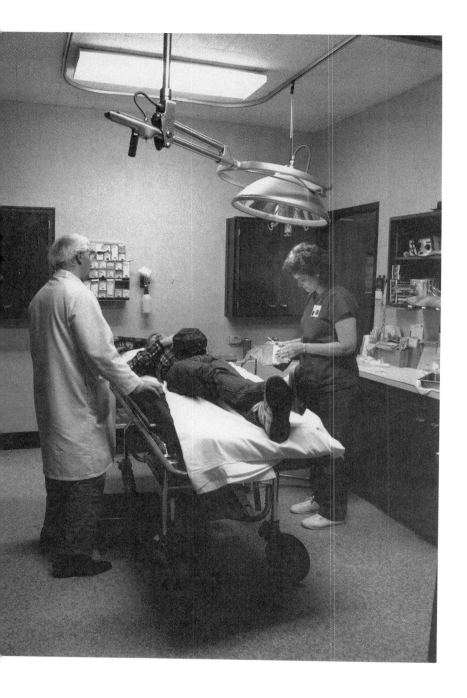

thing in their eye. Also in industrial accidents, someone will be lifting something and hurt their back. We see drug and alcohol overdoses, blackouts, heart attacks, strokes. We see a lot of injuries from car accidents — head injuries, cuts and bruises, broken bones.

Things get tense here almost every day. It may not be because of a life-threatening situation, though that's the most common reason, of course. It could be because of the hecticness of the situation — the hurriedness. I pump myself up. I guess that's how I keep going at the pace I go. It's my responsibility, myself or any nurse's, to get the patients in, get them treated, and get them out as soon as possible. So it's not the laid-back, relaxed atmosphere of a doctor's office where you would be going in for a checkup. The days pass fast. It's in-and-out, in-and-out all day long.

Stress can burn people out. It's the being in constant high gear all the time. I work Monday through Friday. I'm here more than I'm away. My hours should be seven-thirty to four o'clock, but since I'm manager over the area, sometimes I'm here earlier. And I don't always leave at four. Sometimes it's five, six, or seven, depending on the demand. We work until the work is done. There is not a schedule. We do what we have to do.

No matter how much you love or enjoy nursing, you get to the point of burning out and wanting to walk away from it. It's hard to completely separate it from my whole life. I am emotionally involved in what I do, no matter how hard I try not to be — and they teach us not to be — but it's hard. So when I go home, I can't completely forget about the day. And then I'm right back in it the next day. It's a hectic pace. It's stressful. Nurses have to be fairly strong, emotionally and physically.

I feel like I can handle almost anything now. But I can't get too confident either. There are always opportunities to learn more. Nursing is more than I expected it to be. But even after having done it now for fifteen years, I can't think of anything I would rather do, and I don't think too many people can say that. Not in any profession, and especially not in nursing! I love every bit of it!

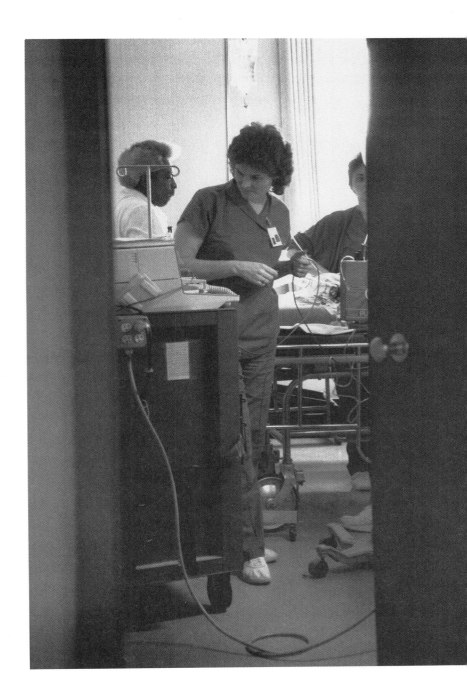

# CHUCK HILT

### ♦ Assembly-line Worker

I get satisfaction out of seeing one of our trucks in a parking lot. I get a kick out of seeing the product that we built. I find myself wondering what job I was doing when that one was built, if I was putting in door pads or windshields or whatever.

*Chuck Hilt works in a large factory that assembles pickup trucks. His job as a "floater" is to fill in for absent or late workers, doing whatever job is needed that day. He attaches various pieces to the unfinished trucks as they move slowly along the assembly line past each worker's station. He loves sports and coaches his union's basketball team.*

◆ ◆ ◆

In our assembly plant, we have five different departments: trim, cab shop, paint, chassis, and the final line. Each one of those departments assembles a portion of the truck. Eventually, all parts join at the final line. They create a truck. And that's basically what our plant does: we assemble the parts that are shipped to us. Some things come in preassembled, like seats. They're assembled at other places and we get them in through freight. We bolt them down and create a truck.

We have about twenty-five hundred people working out here. Primarily, I work in the trim area. My team handles all of the glass: the mirrors, the crank-up windows in the doors, the windshields. We lace 'em up. Anything that pertains to glass: the door handles, the inside molding. When the body leaves trim, it goes over and meets up with the chassis, which is the underbody of the truck. That's the engine, the wheels, and the frame. They drop the body down on it, and then on the final line they put the front panels around the engine.

Some people like knowing what they're going to be doing when they come in. They like to know they're going to be on a certain job. And if they work on it two, three, or four years, they become real proficient at it. A lot of people can — through

customers are taking a real good look at the cars and trucks they buy, looking a lot closer than they ever looked before. When they walk up to one of our trucks, I want it to look good. I don't want to have a screw lying on the floor. The first thing they're going to ask is, "Oh, man! What's loose?" I don't want the paint to be looking bad or something to not be fitting right. I want to make sure it's put together right. First impressions are usually the last impressions. I want them to be impressed with the vehicle when they go to look at it — hopefully buy it, hopefully be a repeat buyer. Even recommend somebody else to buy it.

With competition like it is today, we have to be like that. We have to think ahead. We have to want to make a good product. We have to want to be involved in the process and make sure that our work is good so that our jobs last a long time.

As a member of a work team, I've become close with the team members. We joke. That's how I pass a lot of time — keeping a lot of joking going. We pay attention to the job. We don't want to get to where we're joking so much that we let something slide. But cracking a joke now and then, making conversation about something that's going on, talking sports — all that contributes to making time go faster. If I've got a real good rapport with my team, things seem to go a whole lot better.

This work is basically the same as a sports team.

speed and little shortcuts and things — get their job down to where they can sit and joke or whatever while they're working. But I like coming in and doing different jobs. To me, it makes the time go faster. I don't like getting locked in on a job for a prolonged period of time. I'd rather be a floater. I have no problem with going to other teams, working other jobs, or switching to let somebody else run my job.

I take pride in what I do. I like to do a quality job. I like to try to do everything right. Used to be, long time ago, when cars were selling good, you could just about sell anybody anything. Nowadays, with the job situation, money is tight. So

Same concept. Like a football team: you've got a quarterback, linemen, and running backs. When everybody executes and does what they're supposed to do, then the play is successful. That's the same way with building a truck. If everybody puts the part on they're supposed to put on and puts it on there right, then it won't affect my job or the job after mine. It takes a team effort to do that. One person can't build a truck. It takes a whole team. If one person lacks, or slacks, or isn't doing his job, or is not able to get something on, I might not be able to put my part on. And me not putting my part on might affect somebody else. That's why it's important for everybody to work together and make sure they do it right the first time.

My shift starts at five-twelve in the afternoon. I've been working the second shift ever since I came here. It works out well for me. I can accomplish a lot more at home before I come in. I get off at around three in the morning, and I usually sleep until ten or eleven. Then I get up and take care of whatever I have to do. I have a five-year-old girl and a two-year-old boy. I see my little girl each afternoon before I go to work and

all weekend. And my little boy, when I wake up, I spend a lot of time with him. I take him with me when I run errands. I don't have work pressures at home with this type of job. I come in, I do my job, I do a quality job, and when the line goes down, that's where it ends. When I go out the door, I leave my work here.

I enjoy my work. It's something I can come in and do and have fun doing. I get to work with people I like working around, interact with them all night and talk. And at the end of the shift, I can leave here and go. I like the idea of being able to do that — not having to worry about different things away from the job. But basically I like working around people. Usually there's somebody right next to me, so we can talk, and that makes time go by. We can shoot jokes. And if I can come in to the job and I'm not grumpy, and I can keep that level, then that's pretty good. But if I come in grumpy with my problems, then it's going to affect my work or my job. Then I'm going to do bad work and I'm going to miss something. If I can stay level and get along good with my teammates, then it makes the night go easier, it makes the work go better and I do better quality work. And I'm pretty much happy with myself.

# ROBERT TRUDEAU

### ◆ Teacher

> One of the essential things that I like to give students credit for is questioning. I can't imagine a productive world without people who have been encouraged to ask questions.

*Robert Trudeau has introduced students to a variety of subjects including English, history, and journalism, but he has recently concentrated on teaching geography at a magnet high school of about eleven hundred students.*

◆　◆　◆

One of the great things about being a teacher is the personal autonomy that teachers are given in the classroom. Whether I was teaching at a school in a very poor neighborhood, or in a school in a middle-class neighborhood, or at this special school, I have always had a great deal of personal freedom as long as I kept the kids under good management in the classroom — as long as the parents weren't calling up the school to complain repeatedly. I can carry on unorthodox behavior as long as it isn't done too often, I suppose. That is one of the great joys of teaching. The day significant chunks of that freedom begin to be taken away is the day when it'll no longer be an artistic thing. And it's the day I'll get out of the business.

The art of teaching is the ability to have a lot of spontaneity, the ability to customize the class to the children's needs and to the teachers' needs, and the freedom to move around and not march in an orthodox, strict way through a body of material. I'll admit that marching through a body of material has its points, but overall I think that

the flexibility that's gained . . . who was it who said, "The soul of a good class is the quality of the digression"? I believe in that very strongly. If you are a good teacher, you can make your digressions creative enough — it may not *look* like they apply particularly to the lesson at hand, but they do if you are smart about it.

Good teaching is teaching in such a way that students are stimulated to do more productive thinking using a variety of skills: the skills of analysis (breaking things apart) and synthesis (pulling things together from a variety of sources). The skills of composition, of being able to have a quiet room where they can put their ideas down

on paper in a thoughtful way, as well as the skills of being able to make oral presentations to the class. These are all very important parts of a life-long process, and these are among the things that I want to go on in my classroom virtually daily.

One of the fun things about my class — which I sometimes call World Geography and Cuisine class — is our class meal. I'm obsessed with food, and so I understand that the soul of this material is such that you can make a distinct connection between kids and the study of foreign countries if one of the media through which they connect is food. And so we have these class meals. They tend to be hilarious experiences. It's not lunch;

it's a class activity. Soon we will be eating escargot as we study France. And traditionally, this is a time where the kids get all apprehensive and there is a great roar in the classroom when we mention escargot: "I'm not going to eat those!" "Those are slimy!" "Those are yucky!" "What do they taste like?" "I'm going to eat them!" (That's usually drowned out by the chorus of "Yucko!") But at any rate, I think they very much enjoy the idea of the whole experience even while protesting about being not at all interested in eating them.

One of the wondrous things in teaching geography is that the whole world is our textbook. Our material can come from an antique *National Geographic* or *Life* magazine, or it can come from a clipping that a student has brought in. Or it can come from something like a textbook. In my classes the information rarely comes from a textbook. It's usually from something away from the classroom so as to make it the most intense kind of material. I've taught for years without a textbook — just an atlas, teacher-generated materials (a constant flow of those), and the school's and students' encyclopedias.

I pride myself on the fact that if we had a war and the school buildings were all destroyed and we had to meet here and there in little handfuls, I would teach as effectively as I do now. I don't need massive support systems of audio-visual materials and fancy equipment. In fact, my fantasy in life is to walk about the city like Sophocles, like in the golden age of Greece, asking questions and assaying topics. I want to be like those free-lance commercial teachers who were able to charge what they needed to charge based on their effectiveness and their attractiveness as a teacher.

If this whole system that we have now broke down, I wouldn't be worried about it. I feel like I would make an even better living than I do now.

The lack of a large salary is a big downside in teaching for me. The main way I feel the lack of a deluxe middle-class salary is that I can't take

my kids traveling in a way that I'd like to. A teacher longs to travel because it's such a direct mode of learning. I just don't make enough money to take my kids and go for long distances. And I miss sometimes not being able to keep up with the material rat race. On the other hand, I'd miss that no matter what salary I was making.

What I love most about teaching is that it provides me with an environment for constantly learning. I've never gotten tired of reading and adding to my fund of knowledge. Second, I love the interaction with the kids. They keep me alive in a distinct way. And I have in my heart this longing to help other people learn about the world in the same way that I loved learning about the world. I get to fulfill that desire. Not a week goes by that I don't hear from a former student who has something positive to say about the experience they had in my class. What makes teaching is the satisfaction of knowing that you've touched students' lives in a very positive, productive way and that years later they remember it. That is a very, very important part of a teacher's pay. The psychic payment.

It's very important for me not to do something that purely results in a living — money to pay my expenses. It's very important for me to do something that has a lot of soul in it, and by this, I mean something that is an expression of my personality. My work's not simply pushing numbers around. Instead it is affected by me, the human being, by my quirks and strengths. It's also a heart-to-heart thing. Every occupation certainly does have heart-to-heart work in it — even the ones that seem to have the least heart and soul in them actually have heart in them. But there's something real clear and direct about the heart-to-heart life of a teacher with the students. That's part of the soul of the business.